Tinkling Thoughts

OrangeBooks Publication

Smriti Nagar, Bhilai, Chhattisgarh - 490020

Website: **www.orangebooks.in**

First Edition, 2022

ISBN: 978-93-5621-031-8

Tinkling Thoughts

Swonam Kieran Roul

OrangeBooks Publication

www.orangebooks.in

Acknowledgement

This book would have been impossible to write without the supportive environment provided by my college and university teachers. I would like to give special thanks to my university teachers for always encouraging and motivating me to write.

Thanks to Maa, Bapa, Bapil, Auma, Guli Mausi, Ramesh Uncle, Aai, Sanu Nani, Ansul, Binoy and Agnee bhai. You all are my support system.

About the Author

An unconquerable old soul and young mind, pouring her heart and thoughts into pages through the ink of her pen. She is an ardent reader, a passionate learner and a keen observer of life and its experiences, who believes in taking a positive attitude about life's ups and downs.

Swonam is about to finish her Masters in English at a state government university, Gurugram University. She completed her graduation in English from BJB (Autonomous) college, under Utkal University, Bhubaneswar.

Index

Thought - 1

If you settle your mind and know what you want,

Then more than half of your battle is done.

Thought - 2

Me, in between falling asleep and staying awake the last thoughts:

Alright, time to imagine, what my life would have been, like, if I lived in Regency-era English countryside.

(or more fascinatingly by being a neighbour of Jane Austen)

Thought - 3

Admirable, vulnerable and weak traits are possessed by all, and we deeply crave to uncover them only in front of that one person, so that they can get untangled and resolved.

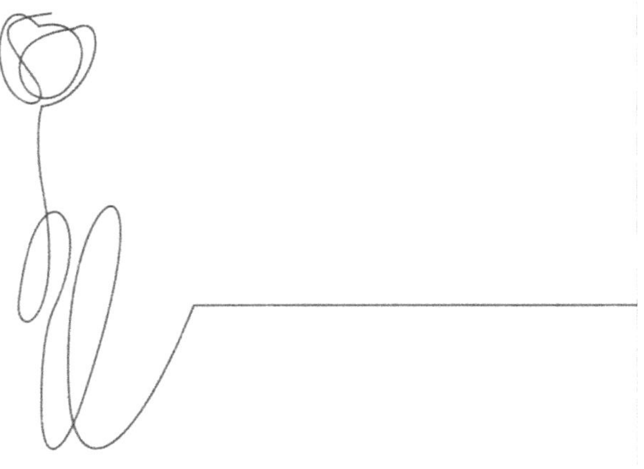

Thought - 4

The seeds of anguish and deep pain, initially I thought were sown by the sudden and ruthless abandonment by you. But, later I realised that it was not because of the departure of such a traitor and betrayer that I was in such a chaos.

But rather, it was my lost soul and wounded heart that I was grieving and mourning for.

However, in this weak female body was laying the faith of a warrior, who bled that sorrow, healed her heart and reinstated her soul back into her body.

Little did you know that the alienation given by you would stimulate her strength with valour.

When will you come and disentangle me?

When will you come and disentangle me?
when will you, too, wish to be disentangled by me?

You and I, both are a beautiful mess,

wandering and searching for love among the
people who care for us less.

Do we, in any manner know each other?

Maybe yes, or no, or think that he/she is just another.

Have we ever had crossed our paths,
where we have seen each other unmasked,

Is a question that my heart has always asked.

Even I am evolving, and so are you,

And silently looking for each other every day that is new.

Tired of asking your whereabouts to the stars,
That when will it start- the story of ours?

I am tired of guarding my heart for so long,
When will you come and make it dance to your song?

I am ready to descend the wall of my heart,
And excited for this beginning and a new start.

I want to find you or be found,
come as early and be by me around.

Even though it rained today, before June,
When will you come and dance to my tune?

I want to be held, cared and pampered by you.
And you also want the same, this I already knew.

So, please come here and meet me soon,

And let's start our romance under the silver moon

We can sense each other out with our strong attraction,
Also, both of us know that we will be each other's
sweetest distraction.

Come here, and disentangle me, And you will be
disentangled by me.

Maa...

A word with countless emotions...

A feeling, very universal and insanely humane
So universal, that its existence is beyond the human race

Animals, birds, any living being
Are capable to understand it

Maa...
Millions of women are united by a single feeling
Over the ocean and around the world

Any race, and culture, or in any part of the world
It feels the same, pure and unmixed.

Maa...
Her scold hides care, care for her child

No matter how big, or small they can be
She loves with every inch of her soul

A child may cry, scold and even misunderstand her

But she, she will hug it all with her compassion

Maa...

A feeling, the deaf can hear And a blind can see

Across the ocean And across the seas

Maa, mommy, mum, mom, mummy

Are all her words by which she is addressed

It is known to all, that she in all names, is the best.

Thought - 5

Moon knows everything.

She will listen to your secrets,

And whisper it in your beloved's ears in his/her dreams.

(And vice-versa)

Thought - 6

Learning is not an end,

It goes on with- Learning,

Unlearning And re-learning.

Thought - 7

Shattering and mending
happen concurrently

It's often from the bottom that we grow.

Thought - 8

Do you really love them?

Or

Do you just love the "idea" of loving them?

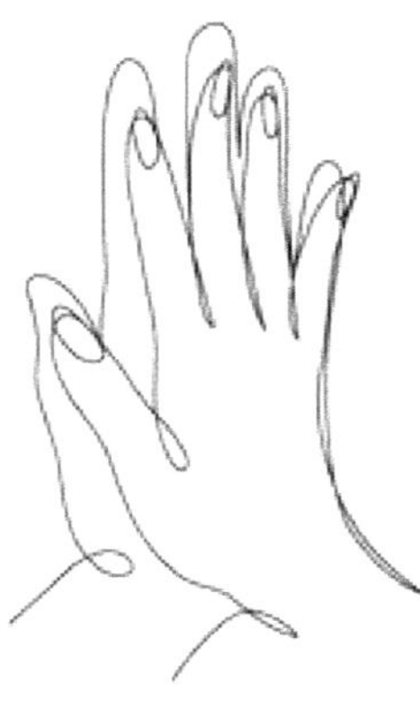

Thought - 9

If our eyes could catch a glimpse of the battles we all carry inside then the war outside would cease.

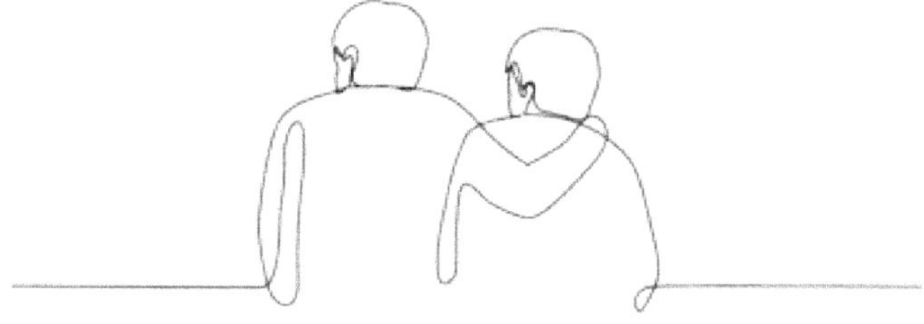

Thought - 10

Sometimes it's easy to bury something in the graveyard of your heart than to let it roam freely in your nerves.

Thought - 11

The thing that is making you wait is also waiting for you.

Thought - 12

When I wanted a knight,

I was forced to pick up my own sword,

And I guess, that's what made me
powerful and strong.

The season will come and will also go

The sun is shining as if it is so high, Oh! No,
not because it is a summer sky.

Gone is the heaviness of the days,
When I wanted to get rid of it in so many ways.

Summer of 69 is all we say,
But every summer brings hope, cheers and gay.

Willing to open up once again,
With all faith as much as I can.

Soon, autumn will come, bringing the dusk,
Before that, hold my hand and have that trust.

This winter, we both won't be alone,
And will take every ride together and
explore what is not known.

Winters are rough and so are we,
If we are once together, then let us be carefree.

The season will come and will also go,
But can we hold each other's hand and forever grow?

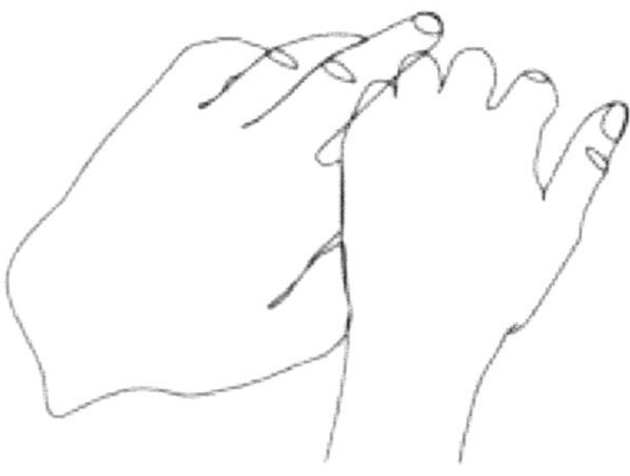

Thought - 13

My feelings for you are making me fly,

With tinkling in the stomach and butterflies in the eye.

Rain and glow

Lazy summers,
Winds so low,
Nature falling asleep,
In the lap of dark night.

Out of nowhere,
You come in,
Soon joy and solace were about to begin.

Rain it is,
That put on the show,
And now my excitement can't stop but glow.

Thought - 14

When our impassive joyous giggles try
to avoid our essence.

How to address it?

Disguising or a coping mechanism?

Thought - 15

Late in the night,
Bleeding the heart out,
No one to see.

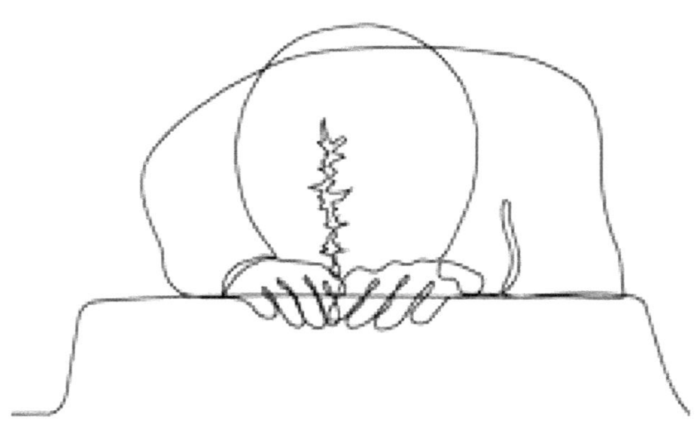

Yes, I...

Yes, I write,
Thinking of you,
That you might come,
And see it through.

There is silence,
On my loud mind,
Looking for you,
Dont I seem mad and blind?

Yes, I am,
Hopelessly romantic,
What else you can expect from me?

Other than also being dramatic?

Desire is there,
To be deciphered by you,
Or else I am keeping low,
And won't accept anyone's bow.

The deepest darkest desire is,
To melt away with your persuasion,
Should I not dream like this?
The world is already rather an utter illusion.

What if it was a blessing in disguise?

We all feel it,
When we enter into
our early adulthood.
The carefree,
the tinkling heart.
Maybe,
we have never felt lively.

We are ready,
Ready
to explore the world,
Without
any guide or a map,
We
just go and run,
Run on the grassland of happiness,
Under
the rainbow sky,
To
catch as much as the breath,
The breath of love, as we can.

We do it,
We find it,

It seems like forever,
So pure, so divine.

Little do we realise,
By seeing the fading green,
That the cold winds are there,
Accompanying the beautiful autumn.

Soon the bubble bursts,
We are in the middle of nowhere,
The green lush turned thorny,
And the shiny sky turned foggy.

So much fog to hide the vision,
Clarity is something that left you long.
You stand there alone, with two friends-
Those are none, but darkness and stillness.

The reality raptures the perception,
Of another reality of sunny creation,
You try to find the warmth of past days,
But winters are too cruel to block the rays.

Will all these ever,
Ever make you doubt,
The blue sky under which you were playing out?

Yes "getting escaped" might be a thought,
to get rid of the winter rot.

But,
Beat the storm, Hold on,
Be there and dont escape.

The warmth you felt,
Was not a lie.

It will come again,
As soon as the winter will die.

Seasons come, seasons go,
If nature is not still,

Then why do you expect a person/situation will stay
according to your will?

Escaping is never a solution. The heartbreak that we all have dealt with, might have changed our perception of certain things.
Did

we use our minds, when the warmth was soothing us? The pain that we are going through right now is just a sign of happiness that is about to happen.

Sun
will shine again. Just let it surprise you in its own way.

What if that hard heartbreak gave you the power to mend a broken heart and a crushed soul?
What
if it was a blessing in disguise that made you inherit the power of alchemy?

Dawn

Enlighten me dawn,
How are you so calm, so quiet,
Peaceful as the middle of the ocean,
Resembling the stillness if I talk of emotion.

No less than a mystery,
Because you will unfold,
A lot of story,
Which are in a lot of ways untold.

Yours are the blue,
That gives us joy,
Because the way you put through,
Even the yellow rays enjoy.

How are you so calm,
By going through the shadiest night?
So soon unlearn and gets disarm,
Like a brave knight after it ceases his brutish fight.

Enlighten me, dawn.

I can't stop praising you,
Seeing what all you have undergone.
How you do this, teach me too.

Thought - 16

Although I am an open book

Still, be my diary/journal and let me spill my secrets to you.

Silence

Silence is the best answer, they say.
Maybe to move you away from their way.

Do you really believe the way it sounds?
Or have diggen up its meaning the other way around?

I am sure, it has many more forms,
Beyond our understanding norms.

- Have you ever felt the silence of-
- Muting your overpowering emotions, which carry a burden as huge as an ocean?
- Holding on desperately when you are about to burst out?
- Silence the urge to confess your feelings?
- Silence of overanalysing the potentially beautiful scenario over and over again loudly?
- Not to burst out the emotion as it can make them (another person) drwon with your

feelings, in fear that it might dent the friendship?

Aren't these sweet, soft and caring?
Even silence has many forms.
Beyond our potentially understanding norms.

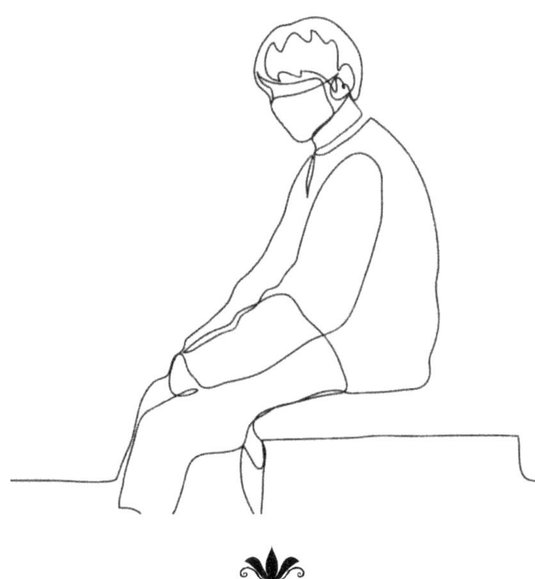

To Ghost You

To ghost you is never my intention
Never before an unfortunate cremation

Even the hatred might grow with every visit
So,don't want us both together to sit

Hidden tricks can't hide for long Before you play it,
you will see me withdrawn

Never thought that you would be so hollow
And am not available for anything that is this shallow

Sense is there that I have seen this before
Don't want to play this game again therefore

Ghosting is hence the safe place to hide
Better than making you listen to my chide

I am done, I am done

Counted reasons to continue, but found none.

Thought - 17

I can feel my heart sinking,
Feeling both full and empty
at the same time.

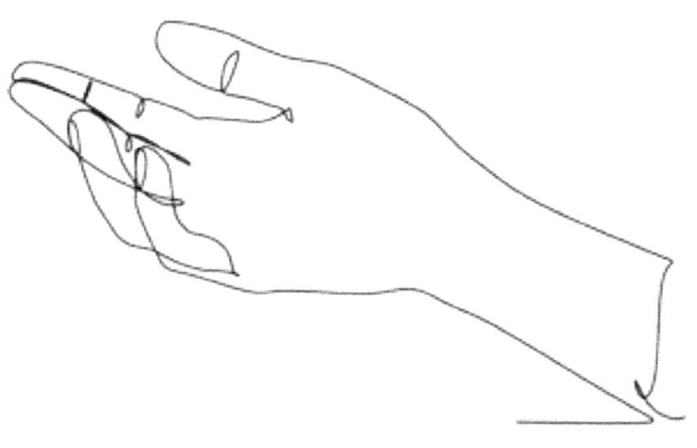

The Sunny Evening

On the sunny evening,
When dusk is no soon to be seen.
I sit alone and think,
What all can I make flow through my ink.

Father has a plan, people say
If there's any good, then where are they?
Behind I see, happy faces or friends
And the time that we all together have spent.

Alone, I sit
No not lonely, not even a little bit
Not even in deep thoughts, I am in
Just a question, when the normal life will begin

Thought - 18

The peace,
Later realised
Was just an
Eye of the storm.

Like a Phoenix, I rise

Kept myself calm on the hardest days,
By putting a smile on and on in other ways.

Loud was the chaos inside my head,
To such a dark "me" I had never met.

Numb was "me" there and there,
Isolating self from everywhere.

Neither sad nor happy was the state,
A ray of hope was too distant.

Puzzled and perplexed was the mind,
But I for myself needed to be kind.

Because there was no one but I,
And like a phoenix had to rise from the ashes and fly.

Unspoken

Where will I take all these unspoken words?
So that it can make me feel less worse.

Unshared feelings turned into grief,
Where to express to get some relief?

Drowned deeply in these thoughts,
With another druther in my mind that crossed.

Uncover it and vent so harsh
Like a hurricane along with a smash

Sorrow would be there in either way,
Because no matter what, they won't stay.

Slaughter this quest, as it too shall pass.
Else you would break again like a tender glass.

Will You Open Up?

Soaked up you are, to think of any relation,
For the past traumas and mental exhaustion.

Is this why you locked your heart?
And keeping yourself so aloof and apart.

Like you, many are there who are shattered,
Whose heart has been mercilessly battered.

What will you do if you meet someone the same?
Who is tired of all mind games which are lame?

Won't it like finding something once lost?
By someone like you, having their path crossed.

Believe again the other way around,
As this world is too big for contentment to be found.

Unable to drop

Unable to drop tears.

It's as if they want to stay with me. To fill the hollowness like a pond of freshwater, to fill the void, that stayed with me after you went. They want to stay while I mourn. They want to feel me while I say nothing. They are not there to immerse my eyes but to gaze at me calmly while I am myself drenched in suffeing and sorrow. As if they are waiting for me till I get exhausted by trying so hard to fix everything. They are waiting for me to see me get crushed in this losing battle. So that those tears can come to my rescue as to what an oasis does to a thirsty soul in the furious, burning and angry desert.

Now you tell, is weeping a thing for the strong or weak?

*Never thought that it would be difficult for me to cry and
let out that ocean of sorrows.
And this brine of grieving wants to stay with me.*

Afternoons

Sunny afternoons,

An afternoon with the chirping of birds and tea,

Tea while reading a book,

Book of a fine taste,

Taste to expand the horizon of the mind,

Mind builds up thoughts, Thoughts to the longings,

Longings of going far places,

Places where I can be myself,

Myself to be unrestricted and bloom,

Bloom radiantly in summer,

Summer has less harsh afternoon,

On that sunny afternoon,
Again I will choose to read while having tea.
This to go on till my ashes are sprouted into the holy
river.

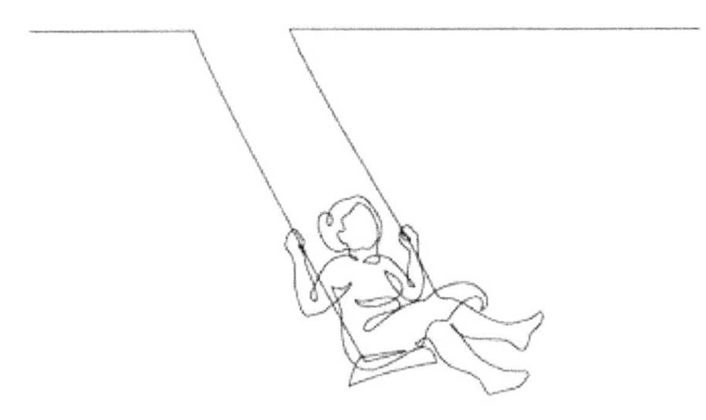

Rain Again

It's here raining again,
The relinquished amusement will be regained.
Dance will my soul to its drop,
To the tuneful carol of its tip-top.

Birds, flowers and even we all hop,
Wanting it not to stop.

Hush-Hush, it is pouring down,
I am lucky, now in my town.

Cheerful within and also out,
We're yearning for it without a doubt.
Sipping tea to exaggerate the delight,
With vintage poems in hands to recite.

Jolly-Molly is the mood.
Acrimonious sentiments are on their way to denude.
This is what drizzle does to me,
It makes me free who is keen to flee.

So, day after day, I pray for rain,
For it drains my sorrows and exempts me from the pain.

Pillow at Night

I hold a pillow to sleep at night,
Because you are not here by my side.

Squeeze it often thinking of you,
Softly making me sleep through.

Every night I feel so hollow,
As if there is something a bit shallow.

Empty spaces beside my bed,
And you are here on my head.

Come out of it so that I can see,
By unlocking my heart through your key.

You will see who the girl is "she",
So deep as saltwater and sea.

Lucky you will feel by my side,
For I won't make my warmth for you to hide.

I will cuddle till the sunrise,
For the entire night till I open my eyes.

I hold a pillow to sleep at night,
Because you are not here by my side.

After a Long Time

After a long time, there is peace,
Glee around and glimmer in my streets.

Thousand times I have seen those dark roads,
Frozen so hard that didn't let me stay composed.

That city had people with fake smiles,
Who tests the innocence of others
and give a devilish trial.
They hide their wicked complexion
with the colour of naive.
To suck your blood as long as you are alive.

Dreadful is the world with such beasts.
Acting like the messenger of love and its priests.
What to do to let such spirits out?
And keep yourself away from such a crowd?

To such thing, letting go is an art,
Cutting off folks who are so dark.
Dark so much like coal,
That naturally repels your innocent soul.

It takes time to show your back,
As you would cunningly and smoothly be hacked.
Once done and off their game,
The existence of that city and its people will become
lame.

So, after a long time, there is peace.
Glee around and glimmer in my streets

Unseen, I Glow

Found world in your vacant stares,
To such venom I was unaware.

Odds of getting immune to your charms were rare,
As the vibe you lent, was found nowhere.

Tonnes of unhappened nostalgic
memories are harsh to bear,
Swimming through it each day is no less than a dare.

Sinking, surging I dare to flow,
Like an unseen pearl in the ocean, I glow.

The More I, The Less I

The more I scream
The less am heard
The more I listen
The less am understood.

The more I am lost
The less am being searched.

The more I please and let others live,
Is less one me to possess a calm breathe.

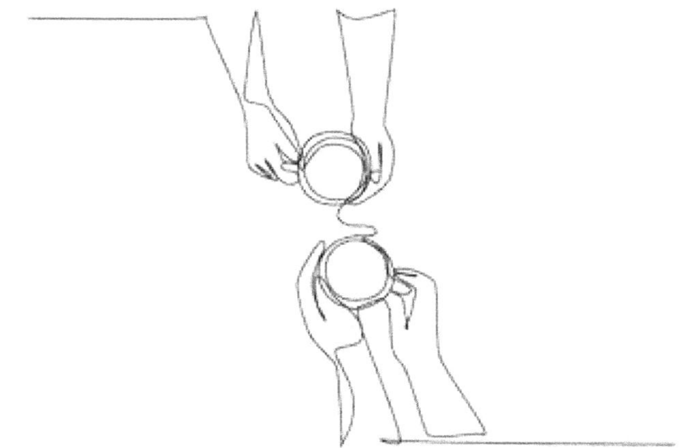

Thought - 19

I know no desire, to not let me get belonged to you.

Can we let ourselves belong to each other?

Déjà vu

Is it true or I am hallucinating so grand?
That is how I ended up in such a fairyland.

Here time is gushing through the clock of sand.
I discern it to be the faith with a plan.

To lay your hand in my hand,
Realised, I, long after it began.

There is something within that's still alive,
Compelling me to realize that I can still thrive.

Like Deja Vu of being possessed by something sweet.
Also, at once, afraid of one more defeat.

Give me your hand

Give me your hand
For I will take you to the land
Where no one catches sight of us
Commencing from the dawn to the dusk

For it will slip soon
My heart says so
Looking at the moon
I beg it to run time slow

Highs and lows will be the way
Where I will never plead you to stay
Till our souls mingle, we'll eat sleep and pray.
To persist it every other day.

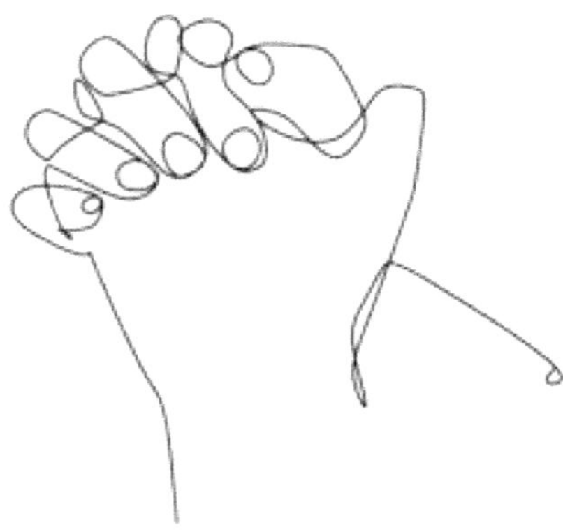

New You

When the moan of the destitute turned into tears of gratitude. After facing the world, that was so shrewd, which was not by any means, less rude to your mood. For its whacked whipping, beating and knocking you down, had always left you bruised and confused.

Little did the realm know, that you would rebound. Again, you found a radiant and glistening ray, for the one that you had once prayed,

"With assorted gloomy days when you will see the light, your eyes will twitch," they said.

Now, with the dampening eyes, numb are you, to conclude that what you are seeing, everything is true. Along with all the things that were thrown on you, but the valiant you, still prevailed through and the vigour within you, helped you grow. Thus deep down, your heart knew that it's a life that's new.

Sometimes I pause and give thought, Are you real

Sometimes, I halt and give a thought,
What a delightful intent life has brought.

Quiet am I, to discern what's next,
To resist any unwanted perplex.

Fair or awful, that juncture will say,
That, what will get unfolded along the way.

Scared and frighten, I think so deep,
As I yearn it to go on without any weep.

When missing you, I can not think straight,
This for you must be great.

Exchanged texts are bringing smiles.
I desire such things to go beyond miles.

Perfect are neither you nor I,
So things can be sometimes low and other times high.

Hiccups when are bound to come,
Then hold my hand and don't get numb.

My heart is racing with the slow beats,
What if this delight from life retreats?

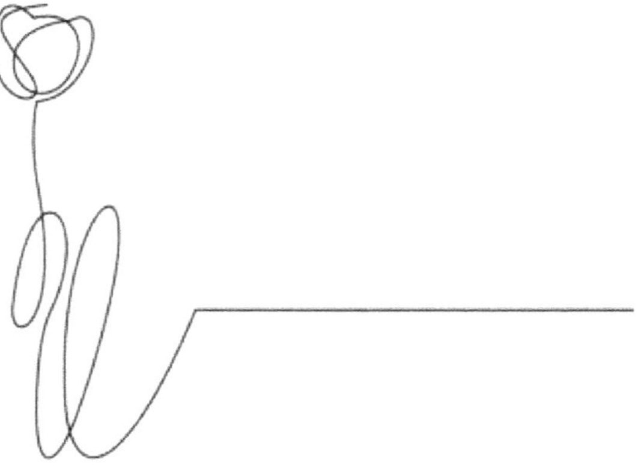

Thought - 20

What if I fall into it passionately that if the situation will go good then fine else I will let myself drown in pain and vomit poetry.

Mornings

My mornings are now, after long sunny
No, not only for the sun but you honey

The smile on the face is now with a calm
And no more about covering up the past harms.

I feel like looking deep into your eyes,
But the distance is there of thousands of miles.

See, what your soul has done here,
Imagine the magic can you put while coming near?

Go on and on

There between the curtain when it was June night,
Unaware for my life to be filled with utter delight.

A flash on-screen was still not cheering,
As I was still unaware of your hearing.

25th was the day when our bows were exchanged, Still
was unaware of the feelings we would be getting
engaged.

Slowly, we diffused in the initial days of Aug, When our
ids by each other, were being stalked.

*"Is this the person" was a question in our mind, Because
we never found one of our kind.*

*Don't know when you made me descend my wall. That
wall to protect me, from the realm, I raised so tall.*

*The calmness within you is healing my soul,
Not in parts, but as a whole.*

*Wish it to go on and on,
By applauding the blooming of a fresh dawn.*

Dazed

When the path is unknown
And there's no light to be shown

Standing in the dark feeling the void
Trying to avoid all the overjoyed memories that did
nothing but destroyed.

Clumsy within, still keeping calm,
Hiding from everyone the chilled feared palm

Silence of mine would never be understood,
As all say, this calm and peaceful
face of yours is so good.

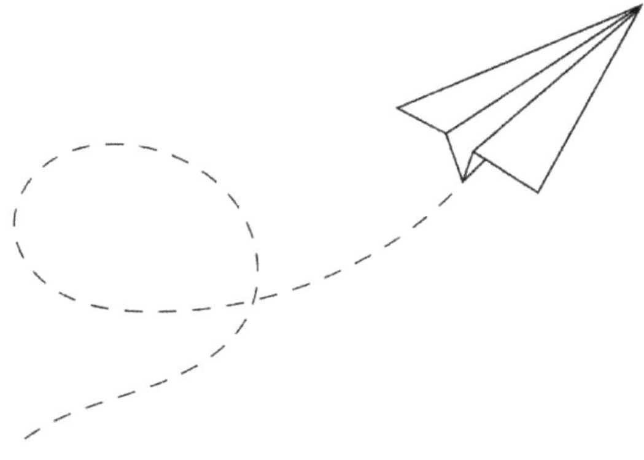

Here I love again

And then there comes a beautiful day,
That enthral your essence with utmost gay.

When the spirits swirl and whirl like anything,
By applauding the moment of the appearing spring.

Like Highs and lows when the heart does lub and dub,
That toss your enchantment to the top.

Blind I go, to that street again,
This time without falling for any man.

Loving the self to the moon and back,
By enticing comprehending with the exquisite tact.

Thought - 21

It's an incredibly sweet pleasure when you feel someone is ripping off the layers of your heart one by one, with their soft gestures, like piercing deep to the centre of the heart after peeling the skin like we peel oranges.

Thought - 22

I have a deep yearning to run my fingers through the knots of your soul to disentangle your mourning.

Kangaroos

I wish to protect you like the kangaroos carry their babies in their pouch. She keeps her child safe there until her child is grown up. I wish to protect you like that. There is no age when it comes to healing. I have been through a lot. A lot of deception, abandonment and bad things. I closed myself completely at that time. And thought that this world is a bad place and people are only sweet when everything is good or when they need something. It took me years to heal myself. I am still on that healing journey. I do get some triggers. Triggers are indicators that there is something within that is needed to be healed. And suppression of it or delaying and ignoring that thing will only make that wound reappear on the surface and I will get far more brutal triggers. At some point of time, I understood that ignoring the wound and suppressing it will only cause me more harm than good. I won't be able to open my arms for the better positive things to come if I will tightly hold the hurt, fear and negative emotions.

This way the world will move forward at its own pace and I will only continue to self-sabotage myself from my own growth.

I don't know what are your trigger points, but I do know that there is something (far more aged damage from the past) that you have become so fearful of and that has made you raise the walls of your guards.

I don't know what is that fear that you are protecting for so long and not addressing. I know you won't tell me.

And I will never force you.

I just know that something is there. So I wish to protect you like a kangaroo protects her baby. I wish to shoo away everything from you that would trigger your wounds until you are healed. I wish to nurture you with care and let your positivity eradicate your negative self-limiting beliefs.

See, I haven't seen you in person, but I am not a fool who can't understand another human being. After all, we both are humans. And although I haven't seen you, still I have this soft corner that has a very deep urge to provide you care and all the nurturing to help

you evolve in your happy and pure state. And in that pouch, I would allow you to have your "me time", even undisturbed by me. That " me time" of yours in that pouch where you can contemplate, look deeper within yourself, have self-introspection and have all the emotional healings. I want my pouch to absorb all your fears, traumatized hurt and a place where you can let go of anything that won't serve you for your highest good. I don't want anyone to dull your spark.

Also, wish you to completely banish the darkness (hurt, fears, self-sabotaging beliefs, negative emotions) dwelling within you.

I wish I could snatch all those hurt from you in that pouch and never give it to you in any other form.

This truth is not hidden and even you know it very well that I have a soft corner for you and that's too tender for you.

I don't want to pamper you like a friend or lover or beloved but as a mother whose actions infuse courage into her child's blood. I want to care for you in a manner that a mother cares for her child. I guess that is a purer form of care and my care for you is not exactly a replicate of a mother's care but comparatively more inclined towards it.

I wish to nurture you with care.

Breakthrough

Winter is howling and marching slow,
Its paleness is glowing through the glistening snow.

Solitary and lone will I stand?
And the frigid breeze will then bite the hand?

Hazy gaze holding a fogging sight,
And chilly violent night approaching
without my gallant knight.

From summer to winter, you were not seen,
I was hoping and fishing for you in between.

On a distant land, you would be looking to the moon,
Do wish the same this time for us to meet by June.

With winters will I stiffen my desire,
For it to melt and ignite with your fire.

Deserted days will pass soon,
Like the waters of the retreating monsoon.

As long the stream, it flows to meet the ocean,
Alike, will merge our emotions with courteous devotion.

For every breakdown is escorted by a breakthrough,
I am longing and yearning, waiting for you.

Words

My mouth needs to be sealed,
As a lot has been already revealed.

So often my jaws make things go wrong,
As it oozes out words where they dont belong.

Better unsaid, unuttered and untold be it,
Rather than committing mistakes on repeat.

Words, behave! You were meant to communicate,
But alas! You (words) are forging detested earthquakes.

Distant

Does it, in an indistinguishable way, ache your heart?
In a manner, I bemoan, we are apart?

Am I the only one persuading joy in my dreams?
Or even you are striving such in the last realms?

Twisting the words to say unearthed,
As brutal might be the violent burst.

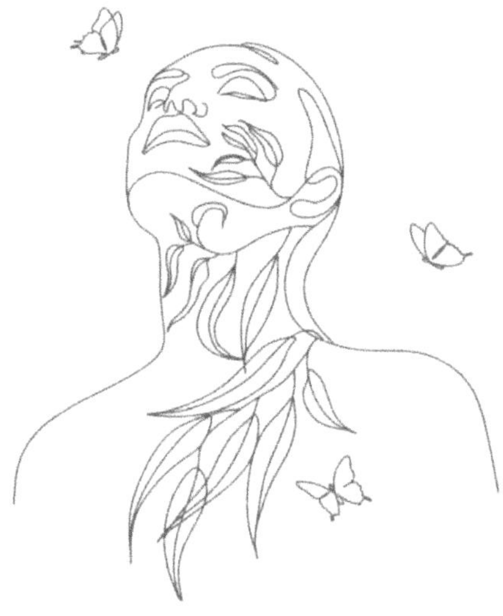

When Done

When I am done, I am done.
Will never go back to make it undone.

Why would I make everything right?
And not see, how from the dark, I glistened to bright?

Why would I not go through a patch so rough?
And not see, how your brutal realm wasn't able to dent
my virtue that's so soft?

Why would I not endure the pain?
For taking wisdom and experience as a gain?

When I am done, I am done.
Will never go back to make it undone.

After a long time, there is peace

After a long time, there is peace,
Glee around and glimmer in my streets.
Thousand times I have seen those darkest roads,
Frozen so hard that didn't let me stay composed.

That city had people with fake smiles,
Who tests the innocence of others and
gives a devilish trial.
They hide their wicked complexion
with the colour of naive,
To suck your blood as long as you are alive.

Dreadful is the crown with such beasts,
Acting like the messengers of love and its priests.
What to do to let such spirits out?
And keep yourself away from such crowd?

To such thing, letting go is an art,
Cutting off folks who are so dark.
Dark so much like coal,
That naturally repels your innocent soul.

It takes time to show your back,
As you would cunningly and smoothly be hacked.
Once done and off their game,
The existence of that city and its people will become
lame.
So, after a long time, there is peace,
Glee around and glimmer in my streets.

Soaked up

Soaked up you are, to think of any relation,
For the past traumas and mental exhaustion.

Is this why you locked your heart?
And keeping yourself so aloof and apart?

Like you, many are there who are shattered,
Whose heart has been mercilessly battered.

What will you do if you meet someone the same?
Who is tired of all mind games which are lame?

Won't it like finding something once lost?
By someone like you, having their path crossed.

Believe again the other way around,
As this world is too big for contentment to be found.

Thought - 23

What lands you in the dar wood is what defines you.

Also, what you do to get out of that dark wood, even that defines you too.

Dark wood: the unrest of your intellect or the awful circumstances you are in.

Light at the end of the tunnel

Slow and sluggish it was striding,
Moments when walking was heavy, but I kept crawling.

Light at the tunnel is coming closer,
Still, time running beyond slower.

Good things take time they say,
This kept my hopes in a long stay.

Summer rays now sing a different song,
Move on, they say, and there is no wrong.

Blowing breeze smashing the face,
Saying there is joy ahead, so go retrace.

84

Good that you are gone

So, was this your care?
That you left me so bare.

Vulnerable to the dark world,
Although it tinkles, but I know its not gold.

"You" the safe place was a myth,
Now if at all any "safe place" exists, to go there would
be the last to think.

Done and dusted when we parted our ways,
Soon happy days started and ended the bad phase.

Delighted, I am, that you are gone.
God sent you in my life, just as a pawn.

So that I can reach my destiny,
By showing my back to all your tyranny.

Thought - 24

This time when I will burst, I want to drizzle soft on your soil, followed by a rainbow, greenery and sunny glow.

I am done bursting like a heavy storm on the deserted lands.

www.ingramcontent.com/pod-product-compliance
Lightning Source LLC
LaVergne TN
LVHW011040200726
843509LV00011B/1315